Beluga Whale

by Rachel Anne Cantor

Consultant: Thane Maynard, Director
Cincinnati Zoo and Botanical Garden
Cincinnati, Ohio

BEARPORT
PUBLISHING

New York, New York

Credits

Cover, © CampCrazy Photography/Shutterstock; Contents, © Serena Livingston/Dreamstime; 4–5, © Miles Away Photography/Shutterstock; 6–7, © Doc White/SeaPics; 8, © J. Helgason/Shutterstock; 9, © Miles Away Photography/Shutterstock; 10, © Volt Collection/Shutterstock; 11, © Campcrazy/Dreamstime; 12–13, © Corbis Premium RF/Alamy Stock Photo; 13T, © afhunta/iStock; 13M, © Jiang Zhongyan/Shutterstock; 13B, © totophotos/Shutterstock; 14–15, © Khep/iStock; 15, © WaterFrame/Alamy Stock Photo; 16, © Yvonne Pijnenburg-Schonewille/Shutterstock; 17, © IDAK/Shutterstock; 18L, © Hans Kim/Shutterstock; 18–19, © Christopher Meder/Shutterstock; 20–21, © nrnaturephotos/Alamy Stock Photo; 22T, © David Shale/Nature Picture Library; 22M, © Lunglee5458/Dreamstime; 22B, © Todd Mintz/Alamy Stock Photo; 23TL, © Khep/iStock; 23TR, © andrey_l/Shutterstock; 23BL, © jim808080/Shutterstock; 23BR, © Miles Away Photography/Shutterstock.

Publisher: Kenn Goin
Editor: Jessica Rudolph
Creative Director: Spencer Brinker
Design: Debrah Kaiser
Photo Researcher: Olympia Shannon

Library of Congress Cataloging-in-Publication Data in process at time of publication (2016)
Library of Congress Control Number: 2015040019
ISBN-13: 978-1-62724-851-8

For more information, write to Bearport Publishing Company, Inc., 45 West 21st Street, Suite 3B, New York, New York 10010. Printed in the United States of America.

10 9 8 7 6 5 4 3 2 1

Contents

What's this weird but cute animal?

Bright white skin!

It's a beluga whale.

4

BIG, round forehead!

5

Brrrr!

Beluga whales live in the cold Arctic Ocean.

They swim in groups called **pods**.

A pod can have up to 200 whales!

a pod of belugas

Often, ice covers parts of the Arctic Ocean.

Belugas are great swimmers.

Their tails and flippers help them zoom through the water.

tail

Belugas can swim backwards!

flipper

Chirp, click, whistle, moo!

Belugas make lots of sounds. How?

Making sounds is how belugas talk to each other.

The whales blow air through their huge, **hollow** foreheads.

Their foreheads are called **melons**.

melon

Time to eat!

Belugas hunt fish, squids, and crabs.

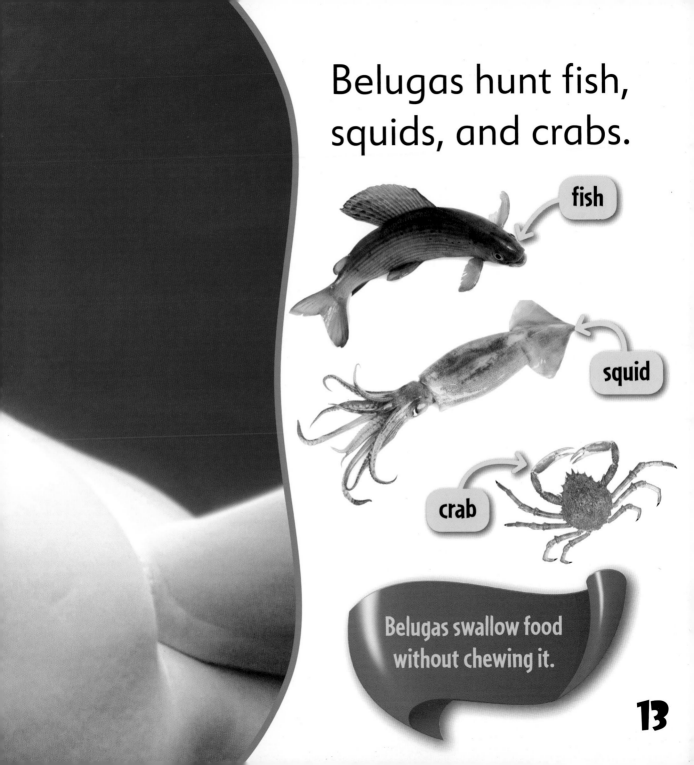

fish

squid

crab

Belugas swallow food without chewing it.

Belugas hold their breath while they swim.

They come up for air every fifteen minutes.

The whales breathe through **blowholes** on their heads.

blowhole

How do belugas breathe when the water is frozen? They make holes in the ice! They crack the ice with their strong backs.

Belugas have to watch
out when they come
up for air.

A polar bear could
be waiting to attack!

Orca whales hunt belugas, too. Orcas are also called killer whales.

Beluga moms give birth to one baby at a time.

A baby is called a calf.

calf

A beluga calf is about the size of an adult human!

Baby belugas are gray.

As they get older, they turn white.

Adult belugas are about the size of a small car!

More Weird Sea Animals

Dumbo Octopus

The dumbo octopus lives on the sea floor. It got its name from the floppy fins on its head that look like elephant ears.

Irrawaddy Dolphin

Most dolphins have long beaks, or mouths. Irrawaddy dolphins have short, round beaks. They live in shallow ocean waters and in rivers in Asia.

Narwhal

The narwhal is a kind of whale that lives in the Arctic Ocean. It has a long, pointed tusk on its forehead that looks like a unicorn's tusk!

Glossary

blowholes (BLOH-hohlz)
openings on top of
whales' heads that allow
the animals to breathe

hollow (HOL-oh)
having empty space
inside

melons (MEL-uhnz)
large, rounded areas
in the front of beluga
whales' heads

pods (PODZ) groups
of whales that live
together

23

Index

Read More

Oldfield, Dawn Bluemel. *Killer Whale: Water Bullet (Blink of an Eye: Superfast Animals).* New York: Bearport (2011).

Rake, Jody Sullivan. *Beluga Whales Up Close (Whales and Dolphins Up Close).* Mankato, MN: Capstone (2009).

Learn More Online

To learn more about beluga whales, visit
www.bearportpublishing.com/WeirdButCute

About the Author

Rachel Anne Cantor lives in New Jersey.
One day, she'd like to sail the ocean to see
if she can find a great white whale.